[ENDANGERED]

LIONS

Written and Illustrated by Daniel Hernández

Endangered Lions

Editors: Jane Hileman and Jayson Fleischer
Author and Illustrator: Daniel Hernández
Book Designer: Robbie Byerly

First Edition, January 2012
ISBN: 978-1-61406-169-4, 1-61406-169-6
Copyright © 2012 by American Reading Company®

an imprint of ARC Press

www.americanreading.com
www.americanreadingathome.com

TABLE OF CONTENTS

PHYSICAL CHARACTERISTICS

Male Lions

Male lions can grow up to four feet tall and nine to ten feet long. They can weigh between 330 and 500 pounds. Since lions are so big, they don't have many **natural** enemies. A lion's fur is yellow-gold and helps to **camouflage** it against the dry grass when it hunts. A male lion's mane is brown and can protect the lion's neck when he fights with other lions.

Female Lions

Female lions are smaller than males and do not have manes. They can weigh between 260 and 400 pounds. Both male and female lions have a tuft of black fur at the end of their tails.

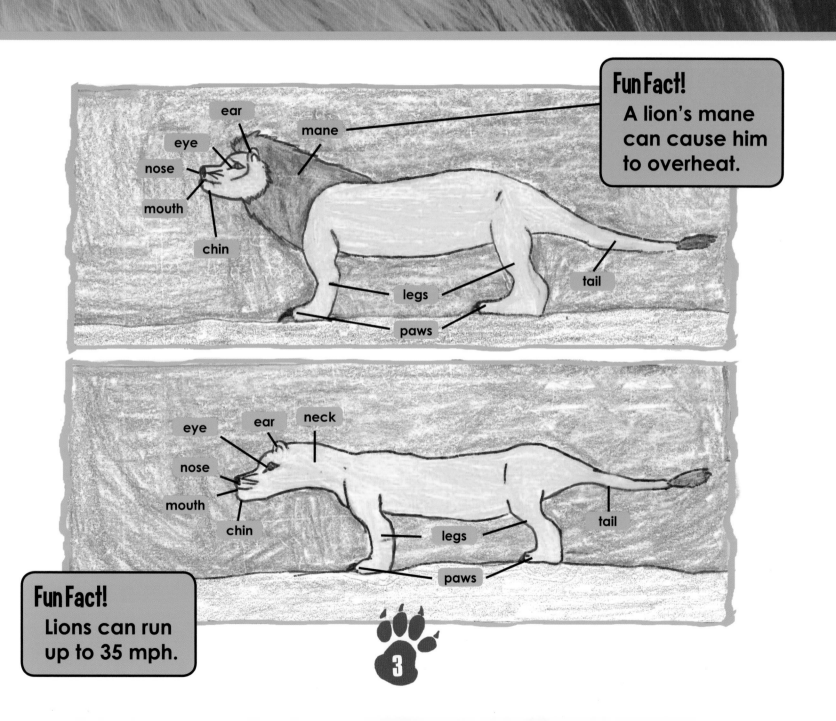

Asiatic Lions

Asiatic lions look a lot like African lions. They have shorter manes than African lions and a fold of skin along their bellies.

Asiatic Lion

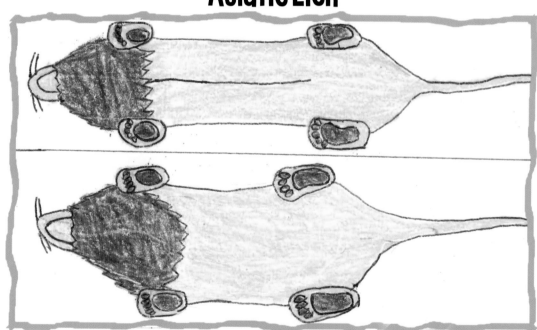

African Lion

Pop Quiz!
1. How much does a male lion weigh?
2. How long is a male lion?
3. What is the difference between male and female lions?

Fun Fact!
Asiatic lions live in the Gir Forest Sanctuary in India.

SAVANNA HOME

African Lions

African lions live on the **savanna**. It is a dry, **desert**-like grassland. There are very few trees on the savanna. This is because there is not enough water to support many trees. The sun is very hot on the savanna, and lions like to sleep in the shade under acacia trees.

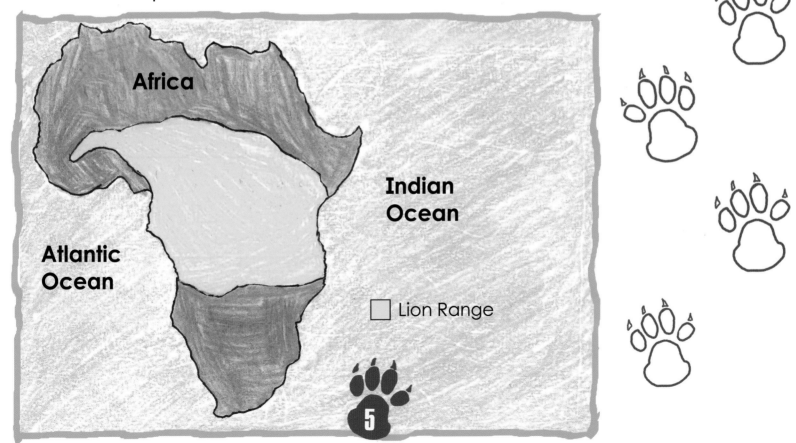

Africa

Indian Ocean

Atlantic Ocean

☐ Lion Range

5

Seasons

The savanna has a dry season and a wet season. The dry season takes place during the winter. It is cooler and has very little rain. During this time of the year, rivers and streams dry up and a lot of plants die. **Herds** of animals migrate to find food and water. The wet season is in the summer. When the rains come, the rivers flow again and new plants grow. The herds come back to feed.

Pop Quiz!

1. What is the name of the sanctuary where Asiatic lions live?
2. What is the name of the tree that lions like to sleep under?
3. Is it hotter or colder during the dry season?

THE CIRCLE OF LIFE

Cubs

Cubs are born in litters of one to six. They weigh two to four pounds and can measure a foot long. Lion cubs are born blind and unable to stand. After two to three weeks of **infancy**, their eyes will open. Female lions will hide their newborn cubs, only bringing them into the pride when they are about six weeks old. Lion cubs start eating meat at three months, but their mother will continue to nurse them until six months. Cubs will begin to hunt at about 11 months.

Maturity

A male lion will leave his pride when he is about three years old. He will live alone, or with one or two other males, until he grows strong enough to take over another pride. When he takes over a new pride, he will usually kill all the cubs so that only the cubs with his genes survive. Lions can live up to 15 years in the wild and 25 years in captivity.

8

Pop Quiz!

1.   When do cubs' eyes open?
2.   When do cubs start hunting?
3.   When does a male lion leave its pride?
4.   How long do lions live in the wild?

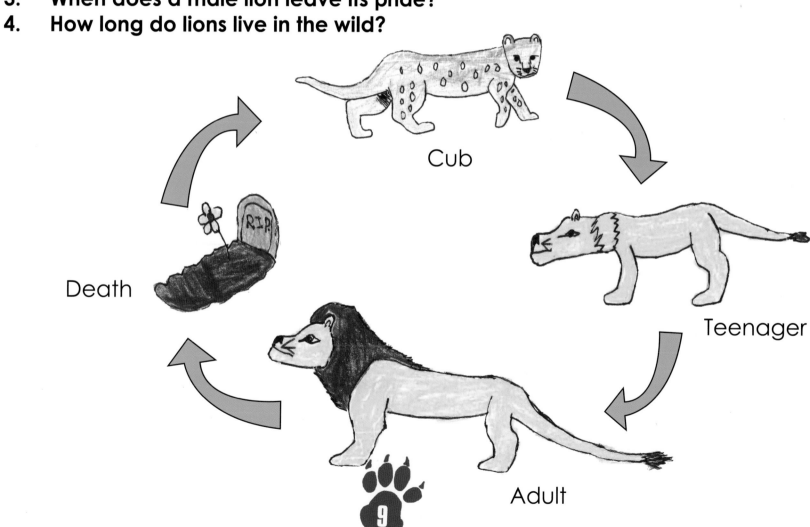

Cub

Teenager

Adult

Death

MEAL TIME

Carnivores

Lions are **carnivores**. They eat meat. Lions usually hunt grazing animals like wildebeest, impala, zebras, buffalo, and wild hogs. They will also eat small animals like birds and hares. When food is scarce, they will sometimes attack elephants. They kill prey by hiding in the tall grass until an animal gets close. Then they rush and leap on their prey, killing it by biting its neck. Lions kill small prey with a swipe of a paw. Sometimes lions will act as **scavengers** and eat animals that have already been killed. Male lions are the first to eat. After they are done, the females will eat. Lion cubs usually eat the leftovers from the adults' meal.

First males eat...

then lionesses...

and finally cubs eat.

Enemies

Healthy lions are at the top of the food chain, but sick and injured lions can become prey to hyenas. Crocodiles will also attack and eat lions, but lions can usually fight them off. Unprotected lion cubs can become prey to hyenas, leopards, and other lions.

Lion Food Web

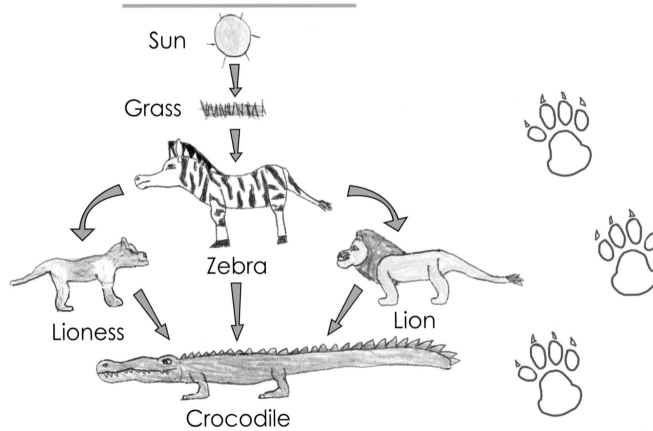

Sun

Grass

Zebra

Lioness

Crocodile

Lion

Pop Quiz
1. What animals will eat lions?
2. What animals will eat lion cubs?

12

BEHAVIOR AND SURVIVAL

Prides

A group of lions is called a pride. Prides can have up to 30 or 40 members. There are usually only about two males in a pride. One of the males is the leader of the pride. He will lead the pride for two to three years before a younger, stronger male takes over. The rest of the pride is made up of females and cubs.

Hunting and Parenting

Female lions do most of the hunting for the pride. Since all of the female lions are related, they will raise the cubs together. All of the cubs will have someone to watch and feed them.

Defense

Male lions are the defenders of the pride. They will mark their territory with scent and fiercely protect it. When intruders enter their territory, male lions will chase them away. They will scare away intruders with their loud roars. A lion's roar can be heard five miles away. Male lions will also use their roars to bring all of the pride members together.

Pop Quiz

1. How many members can be in a pride?
2. Who are the defenders of the pride?
3. Who are the hunters in the pride?
4. How far away can a lion's roar be heard?

14

HELP! I'M ENDANGERED!

Long Ago

Centuries ago, lions lived in North America, Europe, Africa, and Asia. They have disappeared completely from North America and Europe. Even today, lions are disappearing. Thanks to humans, the lion **population** has declined from about 400,000 to about 20,000. The last surviving Asiatic lions live in a sanctuary in India.

Human Expansion

Lions need large territories to hunt in. Humans have taken much of this land for their own use. As humans develop the land for homes and farming, the lions' natural habitat gets smaller. Lions will still try to hunt on this land, and they will kill animals that belong to humans. Ranchers kill lions to protect their cattle. Lions are also killed in traps meant for other animals.

Poaching

Poaching is illegal hunting. It is a huge threat to lions. Most lions live on reserves, but unfortunately even that doesn't stop poachers from killing lions. Poachers hunt lions for their teeth, claws, heads, manes, and fur.

16

Lion Parts Poachers Want

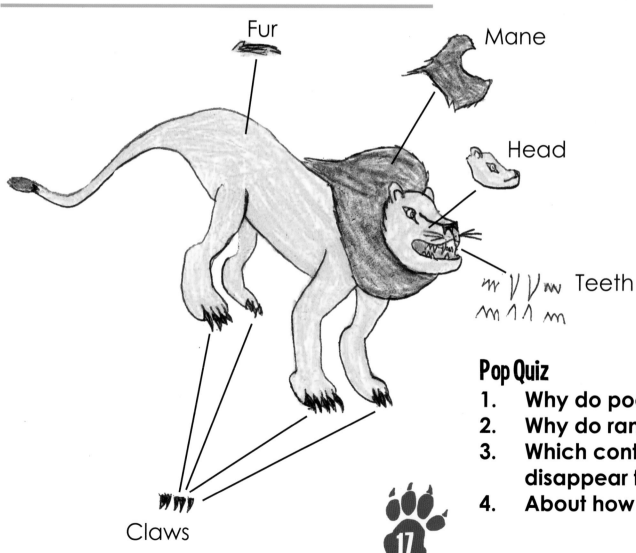

Fur

Mane

Head

Teeth

Claws

Pop Quiz

1. **Why do poachers kill lions?**
2. **Why do ranchers kill lions?**
3. **Which continents did lions disappear from?**
4. **About how many lions are left?**

HELP IS ON THE WAY!

Some people have greatly reduced the number of lions, but many other people are trying to help lions survive. Park rangers and police try to keep poachers from hunting lions. Conservationists try to help ranchers find ways to keep their cattle safe without having to kill lions. One way to do this is for ranchers to build lion-proof ranches instead of poisoning or shooting them. People can also help lions survive by moving some to sanctuaries, where they can be safe to breed. Then they can be released back into the wild. These are just some of the ways that people can help save lions from becoming extinct.

18

CHECK WHAT YOU LEARNED!

Pop Quiz Answers

Page 4

1. 330 to 500 pounds
2. 9 to 10 feet
3. Female lions are smaller with no manes

Page 6

1. Gir Forest Sanctuary
2. Acacia
3. Colder

Page 9

1. 2 to 3 weeks
2. 11 months
3. 3 years
4. 15 years

Page 12

1. Crocodiles and hyenas
2. Leopards, hyenas, and other lions

Page 14

1. 30 to 40
2. Males
3. Females
4. Five miles

Page 17

1. For the claws and teeth and other valuable parts
2. To protect their cattle
3. North America and Europe
4. About 20,000